LIVING SUSTAINABLY

Smart Shopping

Andrew Einspruch

MACMILLAN
LIBRARY

First published in 2010 by
MACMILLAN EDUCATION AUSTRALIA PTY LTD
15–19 Claremont Street, South Yarra 3141
Reprinted 2011

Visit our website at www.macmillan.com.au or go directly to www.macmillanlibrary.com.au

Associated companies and representatives throughout the world.

National Library of Australia Cataloguing-in-Publication entry

Einspruch, Andrew.
  Smart Shopping / Andrew Einspruch
  ISBN: 9781420273281 (hbk.)
  Einspruch, Andrew. Living Sustainably.
  Includes index.
  For primary school age.
  Consumer education—Juvenile literature. Shopping—Juvenile literature. Sustainable living—Juvenile literature.
640.73

Publisher: Carmel Heron
Managing Editor: Vanessa Lanaway
Editor: Laura Jeanne Gobal
Proofreader: Helena Newton

Designer: Kerri Wilson (cover and text)
Page layout: Kerri Wilson
Photo Researcher: Jes Senbergs (management: Debbie Gallagher)
Production Controller: Vanessa Johnson

Printed in China

Acknowledgements
The author and the publisher are grateful to the following for permission to reproduce copyright material:

Front cover photograph of a girl carrying groceries in a reusable bag, courtesy of © Randy Faris/Corbis.

Photographs courtesy of Apple, **13**; The Climate Action Club, **29**; © Rolf Bruderer/Corbis, **3**, **9**; © Randy Faris/Corbis, **5**; © Monkey Business/Dreamstime.com, **7**; © Dmitrijs Dmitrijevs /Dreamstime.com, **6**; © Ivan Kmit/Dreamstime.com, **21**; © Missisippi Images/Dreamstime.com, **27**; © Glenda Powers/Dreamstime.com, **24**; © Christina Richards/Dreamstime.com, **18**; © Moreno Soppelsa/Dreamstime.com, **17**; Earth Friendly Products, **12** (all); George Best/Getty Images, **20**; Ron Levine/Getty Images, **14**; Scott Olson/Getty Images, **23**; Samba Photo/Paulo Fridman/Getty Images, **8**; Peter Ziminski/Getty Images, **4**; © Franky De Meyer/iStockphoto, **19**; © Steve Stone/iStockphoto, **30**; Jupiter Images, **11**; Newspix/News Ltd/Ross Cannon, **28**; Newspix/News Ltd/Rob Maccoll, **10**; Photolibrary © Ange/Alamy, **16**; Photolibrary © G&M Garden Images/Alamy, **26**; Photolibrary © Alex Hinds/Alamy, **15**; Photolibrary/Blend Images, **22**; © Daisy Daisy/Shutterstock, **25**.

While every care has been taken to trace and acknowledge copyright, the publisher tenders their apologies for any accidental infringement where copyright has proved untraceable. Where the attempt has been unsuccessful, the publisher welcomes information that would redress the situation.

Contents

When a word is printed in **bold**, you can look up its meaning in the Glossary on page 31.

Living sustainably

Living sustainably means using things carefully so there is enough left for people in the future. To live sustainably, we need to look after Earth and its **resources**.

If we cut down too many trees now, there will not be enough wood in the future.

The things we do make a difference. We can use water, energy and other resources wisely. Being a smart shopper is one way we can help to make a sustainable world.

The choices we make when we shop affect Earth in many ways.

Smart shopping

If we need or want something, what do we do? We go shopping and buy it. Shopping is how we get many of the things we need or want.

In some places, thousands of people visit shopping centres every day.

Shopping is all about choices. We choose what to buy and where to buy it. Smart shopping choices can help to create a more sustainable world.

Buying fresh vegetables instead of **packaged** vegetables is an example of a smart shopping choice.

Buy locally made goods

Locally made goods are things made or grown near our home. Buying locally is good for the **environment**. Locally made goods need fewer **resources** to get to us.

Sending coffee beans grown in Brazil to other countries can use a lot of Earth's resources.

Locally made goods can be easy to find. At farmers' markets, we can usually find milk, cheese, honey, vegetables and fruit made or grown by local farmers.

Shopping at farmers' markets is a smart choice because food grown locally uses fewer resources.

Buy at local shops

Driving to the shops uses **resources**, such as petrol. The further we drive, the more petrol we use. Shopping close to home means fewer resources are used to get what we need.

Walking or cycling to the shops uses fewer resources than driving a car.

Locally baked bread is fresher and has used fewer resources because it has not travelled far.

Local shops are often owned by people who live in our community. Buying from them means our money supports our community.

Think about who made it

Different companies work in different ways. Some companies try to look after the **environment** and Earth's **resources**. Choosing to buy from them means we are also helping Earth.

Some companies try to look after the environment by removing harmful **chemicals** from their products.

Some computer companies have removed harmful metals from their products.

There are many ways companies can work sustainably.

- They can use **renewable energy**.
- They can **recycle** waste.
- They can use recycled materials.
- They can use less **packaging**.

Buy organic goods

Farms that grow **organic** food do not use harmful **chemicals**. Organic food is better for us and better for the **environment**.

Organic farmers use only natural materials to grow crops, such as these potatoes.

Food is just one example of an organic product. Clothing, sheets and even bath and body products can be organic too.

This label tells us that this T-shirt was made with organic cotton.

Buy recycled goods

Recycled goods are made from things that have already been used. This means that fewer new **resources** are used to make recycled goods.

Used paper can be recycled and made into toilet paper.

Many things can be recycled. Plastic can be recycled into shopping bags. Wood products can be recycled into furniture. Some computer parts can be recycled and used in new computers.

This heap of glass chips will be recycled into new jars and other glass containers.

Buy used goods

Used goods are goods that people do not want anymore. Buying used goods means a new item does not have to be made.

Clothes that we have grown out of can be given to shops that sell used goods.

There are many used goods for sale, such as books, clothes and furniture. We can shop for used goods at garage sales, markets and some shops.

Buying used goods can also be a smart way of saving money.

Think about the packaging

Think about the **packaging** that comes with the things we buy. Most packaging gets thrown away. That is a waste of **resources**. We should always remember to buy products, not packaging.

Toys are usually packaged to grab our attention, but all that packaging goes to waste.

Buying items with less packaging is one way to shop sustainably. We can also buy items that are packaged with **recycled** material. This kind of packaging can sometimes be recycled again.

This logo lets us know that something has been recycled or can be recycled.

Buy in bulk

Buying in bulk means buying goods in large amounts or in the largest size possible. When we buy in bulk, fewer **resources** are used for both **packaging** and transport.

Buying in bulk usually saves us money because less packaging is used.

To buy in bulk, we can go to shops that only sell goods in bulk. We can also choose bigger bottles and family packs when shopping at local supermarkets.

Almost anything can be bought in bulk, including cleaning products.

Tips for sustainable shopping

How we shop makes a difference. Bringing reusable bags to the shops instead of using plastic bags helps the **environment**.

Many people bring reusable bags with them when shopping because some plastic bags cannot be **recycled**.

We can also practise sustainable shopping by planning our shopping trips. One or two well-planned shopping trips use fewer **resources** than five or six quick trips.

Shopping lists help us plan our shopping trips so that fewer trips are needed.

Choose not to shop

Sometimes the best way to keep the **environment** safe is to not buy things at all. If we do not shop, or shop less, then fewer things will be made.

Growing our own herbs instead of buying them is one way of shopping less.

Borrowing books from the library instead of buying them is one way of shopping less.

To stop shopping, we need to find other ways of getting what we need. We can:
- share toys with friends
- grow our own vegetables.

Share the message

Being a smart shopper is an important message to share with your friends. Ask your teacher if your class can make posters about smart shopping to put up around the school.

The message about smart shopping can also be spread by using reusable shopping bags.

A smart-shopping school

Students at Lincoln Academy in Maine, the United States, are trying to reduce the use of plastic shopping bags. They have formed a club to encourage people to use reusable bags.

These students are encouraging their community to be smart shoppers.

A sustainable world

Smart shopping is one way to live sustainably. How many ways can you shop better and smarter? Our choices and actions will help to make a sustainable world.

Make a list of the things you can do to be a smart shopper.

Glossary

chemicals   basic substances that can be used for many things, including cleaning and growing food

environment   the air, water and land that surround us

organic   something that has been made without the use of chemicals and in a way that does not hurt the environment

packaged   wrapped or put into boxes or other containers to be sold

recycle   to create something new out of something that has been used

renewable energy   natural energy that will not run out, such as energy from the wind or Sun

resources   useful things found on Earth that are hard to replace once they run out

Index